"Extremely moving, inspiring, heart-wrenching, great!"

Nathaniel Branden

Psychotherapist and philosopher author of twenty books on the psychology of self-esteem, romantic love, and the life and thought of Objectivist philosopher Ayn Rand.

☙

"*Recession or Plenty: 7 Steps to Success in Business & in Life* is a valuable guidebook for all of us on our journey to success, however we define it."

Frances Hesselbein

Chairman of the Board of Governors of the Leader to Leader Institute, was the Founding President of the Peter F. Drucker Foundation and was CEO of the Girl Scouts of the USA, 1976-1990. Mrs. Hesselbein was awarded the Presidential Medal of Freedom, the United States of America's highest civilian honor, in 1998 by President Clinton. In 2002 Mrs. Hesselbein was the first recipient of the Dwight D. Eisenhower National Security Series Award for her service "to national security and the nation". She is the author of *Hesselbein on Leadership*, and *Be, Know, Do: Leadership the Army Way*, introduced by Frances and General Eric K. Shinseki.

☙

"Marilyn's book follows a principle I use in my work: A concept distilled into its simplest form saves everyone valuable time. Her book is small enough to carry around, yet carries the weight of great thinkers and concepts that not only make sense intellectually, but have also been proven to work. She has created a practical, useful tool full of helpful ideas which are balanced with practical how-to exercises and useful questions.

The tone of the book is friendly. It is like having Marilyn in the room. Give yourself ten minutes here, half an hour there, and read her book as an idea-generator for whatever issues you are facing. With wisdom distilled from her coaching practice, Marilyn's got it right. She clearly has her finger on the pulse of what you need to know today to manage yourself in a small business.

Marshall Goldsmith
www.MarshallGoldsmithLibrary.com
Marshall is a world authority in helping successful leaders get even better – by achieving positive, lasting change in behavior: for themselves, their people and their teams. He is also a *New York Times, Wall Street Journal, BusinessWeek, USAToday* and *Publisher's Weekly* best-selling author of *What Got You Here Won't Get You There* and *MOJO: How to Get It, How to Keep It, and How to Get it Back When You Need It!* , and *Succession: Are You Ready?*.

"As an entrepreneur running a small consultancy business, Marilyn's coaching has inspired me to carry on when things looked tough, and given me ideas for new ventures based on what's in my toolkit, interpreted with her help in whole new ways. Her assistance has been profoundly important to my overall success over the past few years.'

'Marilyn's book does something unique: It brings together some of the most valuable inspirational resources but also practical "nuts and bolts" knowledge that we all need. Her book is helping me in both ways to get through these very difficult times and reach my goals. I credit this book in helping me to thrive not just survive."

Gary Ranker
Forbes Top Five Executive Coach and author of *Political Dilemmas at Work*

"For all the small business owners out there who are struggling in these times, Marilyn McLeod has written a primer you MUST read. It contains heartfelt and hard-won wisdom for all who want to get beyond the mass of information and infomercials they receive every day. This book literally is brimming with enthusiasm while offering clear ideas for success.'

'In this book Marilyn offers practical steps for anyone who wants to start or grow their own business. She does so in a way that is principled as well as reflective. While she channels wisdom from Marshall Goldsmith to Nathaniel Branden, her real contribution is to the business owner. Her 7 principles resonate with the concept that YOU are the most important engine of growth for your own enterprise, and she offers guidance for how you should best spend your precious time, as well as how to think beyond the present in overcoming challenges and obstacles. She offers some great stories to support her points, while keeping the perspective of a coach who is there to help you."

James Goodrich
Founding Dean, Marshall Goldsmith School of Management, Alliant International University

☙

"Intuitive wisdom made practical!"

Kim A. Gutner, M.D., DFAPA
Child, Adolescent and Adult Psychiatry

"Especially valuable during a time of global economic uncertainty that affects all leaders and businesses - small and large - the 7 Steps provides invaluable insights across a set of timely topics. Marilyn's coaching expertise provides guidance in a manner that focuses on you, the reader. She has uniquely assembled wisdoms from great leadership thinkers in a simple to understand and actionable set of stories and exercises. A must read for today's times."

David G. Thomson
Business Advisor to Growth Companies and author of *Blueprint to a Billion: 7 Essentials to Achieve Exponential Growth*

"I have known and worked with Marilyn for almost 10 years. She has always surrounded herself and learned from an eclectic group of the best thought leaders. In her very timely book she shares her personal journey and the journey of others to knowledge and towards wisdom in a very usable way. All we need is the courage, commitment, and discipline to use blueprint she lays out in her wonderful book.

Chris Coffey
Keynote Speaker, Leadership Educator, Executive Coach

"Martin Luther King Jr. once said, 'The ultimate measure of a man is not where he stands in moments of comfort and convenience, but where he stands at times of challenge and controversy'.'

'In *Recession or Plenty: 7 Steps to Success in Business & in Life*, Marilyn courageously shares with us her past personal challenges, and like Phoenix rising from the ashes, provides a road map you can immediately use to be successful in your personal and business life. Marilyn serves as your personal coach by first helping you define the person within you, therefore making it easier to create the world you so desire around you. A must read!"

James Singletary
All-American, former NFL Linebacker, now a Behavioral Optometrist and OrthoKeratologist

"I know Marilyn and well enough that I can actually hear her voice in the book. And it is a refreshingly encouraging voice – never down, always warm and capable of making you see things that you knew but were unable to relate to your own circumstances till she showed you how.'

'She is self effacing but does not mince words and shows you very clearly what you have to do to junk the detritus you carry around with you – often without realizing it! – and start living a life where great things happen to you routinely, and where every day is a blast. This will not happen to you if you merely read the book. There is an excellent chance that it will happen to you if you actually do the things she so clearly and lovingly prescribes."

Srikumar S. Rao

Professor Srikumar Rao, author of *Are You Ready to Succeed?*, *Happiness at Work* and The Personal Mastery Program. His "Creativity and Personal Mastery" course has been so successful at London Business School, Columbia Business School, and Haas School of Business that it has its own alumni association.

Also by Marilyn McLeod:

Conscious Networking
Finding and Creating Your Ideal Communities

Nutrigenomic Diet for Weight and Fat Loss
One Consumer's Journey

Peer Coaching
Extending Your Coaching Dollar

Secrets of Self Publishing
Digital Tools for Publishing and Marketing

Social Media Series:

>***Social Media for Beginners***
>*Step by Step for Small Business*
>
>***Social Media for Small Business***
>*Tips for Using Your Time Effectively*
>
>***How to Work with Your Web Developer***
>*Asking the Right Questions*
>
>***Social Media Strategy***
>*Navigating the New World Online*
>
>***Social Media Workbook***
>*Creating Your Master Plan*

Recession or Plenty

POCKET-SIZE

7 Steps to Success in Business & in Life

by Marilyn McLeod

NOTE: This pocket-size book is abridged. For the complete book, choose the full-size version, compact version, and audio version.

Copyright © 2010
by Marilyn McLeod

All rights reserved. No part of this book may be reproduced or transmitted in any form or by any means, electronic or mechanical, including photocopying, recording, or by any information storage and retrieval system, without written permission from the author, except for the inclusion of brief quotations in a review that includes proper accreditation.

DISCLAIMER:

This publication is designed to provide accurate information in regard to the subject matter covered. The author is not engaged in providing legal, financial, investment, accounting or business advice. Should the reader need such advice, the reader must seek services from a competent professional. The author particularly disclaims any liability, loss or risk taken by individuals who directly or indirectly act on the information contained herein. The author is an independent consultant and coach, and does not represent any of the websites or organizations mentioned herein.

Recession or Plenty Pocket-Size:
7 Steps to Success in Business & in Life

Library of Congress Catalog Card Number

International Standard Book Number
9781451568424

Printed in the United States of America

© Marilyn McLeod 2008. All Rights Reserved.

Rosalind deMille and Olaf Bolm
July 23, 2001
in Carlsbad, California
Photo by Marilyn McLeod

Dedication

I dedicate this book to Olaf Bolm and Rosalind de Mille who began their 78-year friendship when they met at age ten in Hollywood. They gave me a gift of seeing me and accepting me as I am. Though my parents' age, they lovingly included me in their lives as a trusted friend. Olaf, like his father Adolph Bolm, drew out of me the potential he saw by helping me become aware of what I was doing right, and kindly pointing out what detracted. He was proud to hear I was writing this book, as he encouraged me in any creative endeavor.

      Rosalind's response to what I wrote above, "Good." Besides Mrs. Bolm, Rosalind knew Olaf and Adolph Bolm better than anyone. I had the privilege of watching Rosalind read through my first draft, hearing her giggle and watching her turn pages eagerly. She and Olaf both moved to the next experience beyond this life in the months before this book went to print.

Table of Contents

Foreword   xviii
How to Use This Book   xxiii

Section One - **Backdrop**

Ch 1:   Recession or Plenty   2
Ch 2:   Success   5
Ch 3:   Ownership   7
Ch 4:   Image   11
Ch 5:   Legacy   15

Section Two - **The 7 Steps**

Ch 6:   You   21
Ch 7:   Customers   33
Ch 8:   Business   39
Ch 9:   Focus   45
Ch 10: Sales   55
Ch 11: Follow-up & Delivery   69
Ch 12: Review & Celebrate   75

**Personal Management Tools
to Help You Focus:**

Daily Routine   84
Environment   89
Financial Tips   90
Finding Your Desk   92
Focus Session   96
Healthy Exercises   97
How to Use a Planner   103
Needs Literacy   108
Quality Cave Time   115
Values-Based Time Management   116

Feelings & Needs Charts   121
Follow up   129

SEE FULL-SIZE VERSIONS OF THIS BOOK
FOR COMPLETE TEXT AND THE FOLLOWING:

Acknowledgements
Bibliography
Exercise Worksheets
A Personal Note

Ch 13:   Bill – Recovery
Ch 14:   Richard & Sharon – New Roles
Ch 15:   James Singletary – Second Career
Ch 16:   John & Pat Hendrickson – Team Effort
Ch 17:   Daryl – Young and Single
Ch 18:   Adolph Bolm – Second Chance
Ch 19:   Young Marilyn – Without Authority
Ch 20:   Rose, George, Brian – On Their Own

My Mentors:
   Nathaniel Branden
   Chris Coffey
   Peter Drucker
   Marshall Goldsmith
   Paul Hersey
   Frances Hesselbein
   Arthur Samuel Joseph
   Gary Ranker
   Srikumar S. Rao
   Ken Shelton

More Personal Management Tools:
    Coaching
    Peer Coaching
    Creativity
    Open Space Techology
    Project Management
    Twelve Steps

Foreword

During my career, I have had the privilege of working with over 100 major CEO's and their management teams. My clients are already successful leaders who are working to "take it to the next level" and get even better.

I met Marilyn in 2002 when I was looking for someone to create a website for me. "Just a small website," I told her. Not only did she help me create my small website just the way I envisioned it, she also helped me grow it into a significant Internet presence that catalogs my work, and gives my clients and anyone who visits hundreds of articles, columns, videos and audios about the concepts I teach in my coaching practice.

Throughout the years we have worked together, Marilyn has applied her broad range of skills to several new projects and opportunities in my own business. She has shown the highest integrity and has handled a couple of tough situations in a very professional way.

Marilyn has firsthand experience with the Marshall Goldsmith coaching concepts she presents in her book. She recently managed a coaching engagement with four very senior executives in a 'Fortune 500' client of mine. She did a wonderful job of managing the work of coaches involved—and coordinating the project. The end result was positive, long-term change in behavior for the client executives—and a very positive experience for the coaches!

As my coaching clients know, our coaching involves a guarantee … that the person being coached shows documented positive results through a mini-survey. The raters are not me, nor the coaching client, but instead the client's stakeholders. The mini-survey results of Marilyn's own coaching engagements also show documented positive results.

Though Marilyn's coaching has focused mainly on small business owners during her career, the exercises and concepts she presents in her book make sense for anyone who is taking charge of their own enterprise, their career, or finding their way through a personal challenge or transition. The 7 Steps she presents offer tools to improve anyone's personal management skills.

As I read through her book, it was interesting to learn more about her background, and what informs her coaching. Marilyn is an exceptional coach. She has a way of fitting into an environment and providing support and guidance in a manner that does not call attention to herself, but instead enhances the business owner's vision and personal style.

This book is being published during a time of global economic uncertainty. The topics are timely. Marilyn has brought together the wisdom of some of the greatest leadership thinkers in modern times, including several of my own mentors, and created a very readable resource book of tools which are especially vital in our changing environment.

Marilyn's book follows a principle I use in my work: A concept distilled into its simplest form saves everyone valuable time. Her book is small enough to carry around, yet carries the weight of great thinkers and concepts that not only make sense intellectually, but have also been proven to work. She has created a practical, useful tool full of helpful ideas which are balanced with practical how-to exercises and useful questions.

The tone of the book is friendly. It is like having Marilyn in the room. Give yourself ten minutes here, half an hour there, and read her book as an idea-generator for whatever issues you are facing. With wisdom distilled from her coaching practice, Marilyn's got it right. She clearly has her finger on the pulse of what you need to know today to manage yourself in a small business.

— **Marshall Goldsmith**

Marshall Goldsmith

New York Times, Wall Street Journal, BusinessWeek, USAToday and *Publisher's Weekly* best-selling author of :

> *What Got You Here Won't Get You There* (Hyperion)
>
> *MOJO: How to Get It, How to Keep It, and How to Get it Back When You Need It!* (Hyperion)
>
> *Succession: Are You Ready?* (Harvard Business Press)
>
> *The Organization of the Future 2* by Frances Hesselbein and Marshall Goldsmith (Jossey-Bass)
>
> *Leader of the Future 2* by Frances Hesselbein and Marshall Goldsmith (Jossey-Bass)

www.MarshallGoldsmithLibrary.com

How to Use This Book

Quick Summary:

• This book is written to be as usable as possible.

Exercise:

1) Decide how you are going to use this book:

- Reference book when you need new ideas
- Study guide by yourself or with your coach
- Improvement guide for your team, family, support group

2) Create time in your schedule to follow through with your intention above.

3) Is there anything in the way of you following through? If so, address this as best you can to support the improvement you want.

4) Send me an email occasionally to let me know how it's working for you! You will find the book website at http://www.CoachMarilyn.com.

How to Use This Book

☙

I won't mince words. This book is about courage. It's also about the tools I've found that have helped me get through the tough times. I will introduce you to some of my mentors whose friendship and wisdom have been a valuable component of my success thus far.

This experience we call life is not for the faint of heart. It takes courage to get up every day and face what cannot help on some level being unpredictable. Some people thrive on the adrenaline rush of the unexpected, enjoying the hunt. Other people create as routine and safe an existence as possible. We are all different people, and we each embody our own array of unknowns: our health, our mood, our choices.

I'm hoping you will become aware of the choices you have been making that affect your options much more than you know, and that you will take that awareness and make informed choices about situations and conditions that affect your life and the lives of those around you.

If from that conscious perspective you choose to live a life others (or even you) may have judged as ineffective or unflattering, I'll get in your corner and be your champion. I will trust you're making your best choice for the moment, and that as you see a better choice in the future, you will be ready to make another choice, or a series of other choices, either gradually or suddenly, as it makes sense for you.

The point is ... it comes from within you. My statements are only suggestions!! I won't tell you what to do, and I hope you don't let anyone else tell you what to do. It's your life. I hope you look within yourself to find your deeper truth, and make your own decisions.

I've written a reference book that I intend to use myself! Please take what works for you and discard the rest. Here's to courage as we share the journey together! I've organized this book so it can be used in a variety of ways:

Greater Depth
This book is intended to be an idea-generator, reference, and comfort food for the soul. I provide resources and urls in the book and on the website if you want to study any of these concepts in greater depth.

You can take this journey in several ways:

• Read the book and do the exercises by yourself.

• Ask a friend to read the book with you and do the exercises together.

- Start a group to study the material together and support each other as you try out the exercises.

- Visit the book website and join others who are reading the book, sharing your experiences and tracking your progress online. www.CoachMarilyn.com.

- I've included the complete bibliography online with easy links to help you find the materials.

Building a Future
Is it your birthday, or January 1st, or have you just had a major life change and you're thinking about what direction to take next? This book can help you sort out your options, and help you focus on a future plan.

As you're reading the book, I recommend:

- Take time to consider how these ideas and questions relate to you. Take as much time as you need. Start a journal and write down your impressions in phrases so you can remember later. Just take notes about your thoughts. They don't all have to make sense yet.

- If you feel you need more information to answer the questions, wander through the book either by looking up key words in the index at the back of the book, looking at the charts (page 121), or reading a story in Section Three (see full version of this book).

• Change and transition can sometimes be lonely or daunting. Many people find that creating a routine in their lives helps them move forward. Most people seem to make more consistent progress toward their goals when they're accountable to someone besides themselves.

Some Suggested Routines:

• Choose a time of day or a day of the week to read the book and do the exercises, and stick to your schedule.

• Are you hearing your friends or business associates making the same old negative comments over and over again? Are you looking for a positive environment that will help you trust in yourself and your future? Consider starting a study group, where everyone gets together once a week to discuss the section of the book they've read and applied between meetings.

• To create more accountability, ask someone you trust will be honest and fair with you to be your peer coach. Tell them what you plan to do and when, and schedule a regular time to check in with each other about the goals you set for yourselves. You can help each other stay on target. See Peer Coaching in the full version of this book.

• You may be one of my coaching clients or a student in one of my courses. If so, please do the homework and let me know how things are going for you. I can only help you if you tell me what works and what doesn't.

I am always interested in learning new ideas! I'm sharing the best of what I've learned so far, and I expect you'll build on what you learn in the book. Let me know what you've discovered and invented as a result of being inspired by my book! It's like having grandchildren … I don't have to go through labor or pay for college … I just get to see traces of my labors of love reflected in your wonderful creations. That is my real payback … to see how you have used what I offer.

Marilyn McLeod
San Diego 2010

SECTION ONE

Backdrop

"Whatever you can do, or dream you can,

begin it.

Boldness has genius, power and magic

in it."

(attributed to Goethe)

CHAPTER 1:

Recession or Plenty
ఴ

Quick Summary:

• Fortunes, health and advantages come and go.

• Develop a range of strategies to respond to evolving conditions.

• Often the seeds of our solutions are in plain sight. It takes creative thought to uncover important assets we may have missed.

• To get out of a rut, it helps to understand areas of weakness honestly, and then to focus on where you want to go.

• Character wears well in any condition.

Exercise:

1) Make a list of your current reality: One list of what you like about your life and business now, and the other list of what you don't like.

2) Look honestly at both lists, and begin to create a vision of what you truly want that resonates deeply with the truth of who you are.

3) Step out of any mental constructs such as anger, judgment, criticism, diagnosis, blame and resentment. From that point of clarity, look at your 'don't like' list again. Are there people and resources on that list who could help you if you approached them in a positive, supportive way?

4) Write down any new perspective you now have about your own definition of recession and plenty.

☙

CHAPTER 2:

Success

෩

Quick Summary:

• Everyone has their own definition of success and their own reasons for being in business.

• For better or worse, we often impose our own definitions on other people.

• Sometimes finding our authentic path to success and happiness involves being willing to look at new ideas, and try new things.

• Getting past the stigma of being wrong has immense benefits.

Chapter 2: Success

Exercise:

1) Write down your own definition of success. Now think of someone who loves you unconditionally, without regard to your material or social success. From their perspective, read the definition you've just written down. Does it ring true as your own?

2) Do an experiment to find out more about yourself. Think about something you have strong feelings about, and then ask some people for their ideas about this topic. Watch how you respond. Do you notice yourself reaching for a pen to write down the new ideas you're learning, or do you hear yourself defending your deeply held convictions?

3) If you heard yourself talking defensively, stop and notice what you are saying to yourself right now. Are you berating yourself for doing something wrong, or are you giggling in loving amusement because you caught yourself doing something silly again?

ℰℑ

CHAPTER 3:
Ownership
☙

Quick Summary:

• Ownership is a multifaceted concept.

• Ownership in a small business means wearing many hats, including boss and employee.

• We are better equipped to run our own business when we take responsibility for our own decisions, and management of our own resources.

• Blame and excuses are expensive.

• Self-motivation, self-responsibility and clear, objective vision are like gold.

• When considering taking on a partnership, consider carefully, and then think it over again.

Chapter 3: Ownership

Exercise:

1) Think about yourself and your reasons for wanting to be in business. Write down your thoughts.

2) Think about who you want to share ownership with, and why. Write down what you expect each owner to contribute, and what you think the business owes them. Beyond the money, are there intangibles involved?

3) Think about the functions you expect your enterprise will require to run. Which functions are supplied by an owner, and which will you hire out? Try to clarify everything. (Your ideas may evolve as you read the 7 Steps in this book.)

4) Look at the list of people you plan to involve in your enterprise. How much do you really trust them? Have they demonstrated integrity and dependability in the past? In what ways can you not count on them?

5) Now look at yourself and apply the same standards to yourself. Can you really count on yourself to carry out your part of this business?

Make a list of improvements you would like to see in yourself and everyone else involved before you move forward.

☙

CHAPTER 4:

Image
℘

Quick Summary:

• The image that really sells has less to do with the cost and flashiness of your promotional materials, and more to do with:

  • The depth of personal authenticity you convey, and

  • How much you sincerely care about the other person's wellbeing.

• To convey mastery of your business message: practice, practice, practice.

• Sincere appreciation of others can be the most powerful incentive program.

Exercise:

1) Can you convey your message effectively without PowerPoint?

2) The next time you're in front of a prospective customer or stakeholder, notice how you're coming across:

> • Do you push your 30 second commercial at them whether they want it or not? When you do this, how often does this lead to a new customer?

> • Do you listen first to understand who you are talking to and what they need? When you do this, how often does this lead to a follow up conversation?

3) Ask people around you (who will tell you the truth) how often you let them win, and whether they consider you a good listener.

4) Think about your presentation from your ideal customer's point of view. What about image would turn them on, and what would turn them off?

"Be so good they can't ignore you."

Steve Martin
Comedian, Muscian, Actor

CHAPTER 5:
Legacy

❧

Quick Summary:

• Thinking about the legacy we want to leave helps us balance short-term thinking with what lasts.

• Getting beyond the paradigms of winners and losers, who belongs and who are the outsiders, and who is right and wrong, helps us bridge current challenges to paradigms that work cross-culturally and over longer periods of time.

• What we do each day and how we live our lives may be more powerful than any legacy planning.

• Part of being successful is giving back.

Chapter 5: Legacy

Exercise:

1) Try Marshall Goldsmith's exercise: 95 year old man or woman (page 156).

2) Think about what matters to you and your customers and stakeholders. Is there a contribution you can make to your local community to address a need in this area?

3) Think about where you came from, and how people still in that situation may be struggling. Is there something you can do to make life easier for them, or to help them succeed?

4) Think about what you've learned during your life and career. Is there something you can package and turn into a gift or product that could help others?

ஓ

© Marilyn McLeod 2008. All Rights Reserved.

SECTION TWO

The 7 Steps

This section is about starting a new small business, or becoming more successful in your small business. The principles can be applied to other projects and situations; I will let you decide what fits and what does not. I've included some stories that illustrate various points of view.

If you're thinking of starting a new business of your own, you may think first of the skills you have that could be marketable. That is an important consideration, but it's not where I start. You can't just quit and walk away from your own business as easily as you can quit and walk away from a job. If you're going to create a role for yourself that you'll be living with day in and day out because you own the business, then I think it's highly valuable to create something you will enjoy doing day in and day out for years!

So I start with **YOU**:

Step 1:   **You**
Step 2:   **Customers**
Step 3:   **Business**
Step 4:   **Focus**
Step 5:   **Sales**
Step 6:   **Follow-up & Delivery**
Step 7:   **Review & Celebrate**

CHAPTER 6:
You
ಌ

Quick Summary:

• Who runs your engine? As a small business owner, you are the most valuable resource your business has. Without you, nothing in your business happens.

• Your health and happiness are a primary consideration in the long term success of your venture.

• Creating a life close to your values helps your happiness level.

Chapter 6: Step 1: You

Exercise:

1) Think about you and what really makes you happy. Write down specifics that come to mind.

2) Think about times you feel stifled, discouraged, uncomfortable. Write down the situations that stimulate this feeling, and what specifically you don't like about it.

3) Think about yourself and all that you are. What aspects of yourself that make you happy remain untapped?

4) If you could have an ideal day, an ideal job, an ideal customer, an ideal life, what would it be like? Dream, and take notes!!!

Step 1: It IS About You

Accept that you are the one who must champion your new creation.

You may think your product or service is your starting point, but your key is closer to home. You are the one who will be putting in the long hours to bring your vision to fruition. You have to be healthy to carry this responsibility, and you have to be happy to carry it long enough to make it work.

What makes you happy? What do you especially enjoy doing, and who do you most like to spend time with? What are your values? What roles most appeal to you? Define a role, career, product or company that matches who you are authentically as closely as possible.

Chapter 6: Step 1: You

Your Business Engine

What is the most important factor to your success as a sole proprietor, and how can you take very good care of this factor?

Think back to a time you felt really 'on'. Was it a situation where you were in charge, knowing just what to do, directing people and resources effectively to the right places, and the situation resolved smoothly into a positive result? Was it a time your fans listened adoringly as you explained the key concepts of your new project? Think of the situation, and look at which of your needs were getting met during this experience. Refer to the Needs Chart (page 121).

Now think of a situation that did not feel good at all. Was it a time when you didn't know the answer? Were people not responding as you expected them to? Were you unable to make the progress you were hoping to make, or did you get bad news that seemed to undermine everything you'd been working toward, or that you stood for?

Chances are, if you look at which needs were not getting met in the second situation, they probably have some similarity to the list you made in the more comfortable situation when you felt strong and good. Two sides of the same coin. Tuck the list away for future reference. It's just good to know what some of your needs are.

How well do you know yourself, and do you really know what makes you happy?

Jack Weil was Founder and CEO of Rockmount Ranch Wear. When people asked him what advice he would give young people starting a career, he would say, "Love your job. If you don't, change jobs, because nothing is worse than the drudgery of a job you don't like." For him, his work was his second romance, next to his marriage. Jack Weil died at the age of 107 on August 13, 2008. His grandson, Steve Weil, said of him: "He kept working all the way up to the end. He was a very inspiring person, and quite frankly, he seemed like he was in his 60s when he got into his 90s."

Marshall Goldsmith, leadership coach to top CEO's internationally, asks the question, "Who are you, and how do you know?"

You can probably recite for me whether you had a happy or difficult childhood, where you went to school or the opportunities you missed, what kind of work you do, something about your family, what your hobbies are. This tells me something about you, but it's not the deeper story. You might look at Marshall's book *MOJO: How to Get It, How to Keep It, and How to Get it Back When You Need It!* (Hyperion) to explore this topic further.

Chapter 6: Step 1: You

Your Most Valuable Resource

If you are like most ambitious people who start their own business, you are driven and resourceful and you will keep going until you get the job done. You probably focus more on the task at hand than on the person doing the task at hand. You just want this task to be complete so you can put on another hat and take care of the next task.

I want you to look around your office and think about the machines your business depends on. Would your business run if you didn't have a computer or a telephone? What happens when something goes wrong with them? Everything stops until you get them fixed so you can get back in business!

Now, think about the 'machine' that runs those machines … your body! How well would the computer and telephone work if you were not there to use them, to make decisions about how to use them, to prioritize the work and get new clients and – and – and … ?

As leader of your business, especially as a sole proprietor, your good health becomes vital. When you don't work, your clients don't receive what you've promised them, and you don't get paid.

How can you take better care of your most precious resource and still keep up with the schedule required to keep it all going? How do you take good care of your health?

You've heard it before … exercise, get plenty of rest, drink water, take food supplements, avoid junk food, be happy. Just do it!

Maybe you're like me and you think you're cheating nature because you can stay up all night and drive yourself better than the people around you - maybe you can, and maybe it won't catch up with you. Personally, I found there was a limit to how hard I could push myself without replenishing my resources. I still keep pushing for more achievement, but I've included in my list of tasks items that keep my body healthy and strong, and activities that feed my spirit.

Back to you and what you enjoy. Here are some questions that I've found help my clients create the kind of business they will enjoy over time:

- Do you prefer to work **on your own** or **with a team**?

- Do you like to **follow a set structure** and follow the rules, or do you prefer to **create your own style** and your own rules?

- Do you appreciate **close supervision** or are you more **self directed**?

- Do you like to **set goals ahead** or just **follow your intuition**?

- Are you more comfortable having just **one product** or a **variety of options**?

- Do you **love to sell** or **hate to sell**?

- Do you prefer to **hit the ground running** or **ease into it**?

- Are you more comfortable calling on **people you already know** or a **cold market**?

- Are you more in your element in a **residential** market or a **commercial** market?

- Do you like to **follow a proven system** or **customize a system** to match you personally?

There are no right answers; only what fits you today. It may change tomorrow. It's just important to know yourself, and to be honest with yourself about what you sincerely enjoy.

Backup

You're probably the only one qualified to handle the myriad array of tasks you juggle each day to keep your enterprise going. You probably can't stop long enough to think about what would happen if you didn't show up one day. Take a moment anyway and think about this. Create backup plans. What are some strategies to keep things going if you have to step away for awhile?

It's All About You

You make your own choices, even if they're small. No one really can be in your shoes; you are the complete expert on you. Other people, like coaches, have some good ideas. Be a smart consumer and make your own choices about the ideas you implement.

Consider the possibility that you might know something about making good choices for yourself, and start small, building your confidence. Will you make some mistakes? I prefer to think of them as choices I make that give me more information so I can make different choices next time. How can you learn if you don't make

Chapter 6: Step 1: You

choices? The more choices you make, the more times you'll miss the mark, but the better you'll get at knowing where your target is and how to get there.

♪

"If I could have half the things I've talked myself out of, I'd be a very happy man."

Colin Gautrey
Author, Coach and Facilitator Specialising in the practical use of power and influence in the workplace.
Political Dilemmas at Work
www.PoliticsAtWork.com

CHAPTER 7:
Customers
℘

Quick Summary:

• You can choose your customers.

• You can change your customers.

• Find customers you really enjoy being with. This will make it a pleasant experience to serve them, because you'll want to help them anyway.

Exercise:

1) Think about who you enjoy spending time with. Write down any specifics that come to mind.

2) Are there particular activities you enjoy doing with these people, and others that you don't like doing with them? Think about this and take notes.

3) What kind of people do you naturally attract? Are they people you enjoy being with? If yes, what do you like about them? If no, what don't you like about the interaction? Can you think of a way to make this win-win? Take notes.

Step 2: Your Customers

Clarify: Who is your customer?

Spend some quality time with the people you most enjoy being around and listen to them on their terms. Learn what they need, and from that perspective start thinking about what valuable improvement in their lives you can provide.

A 'customer' is more inclusive than just the people you are hoping will buy what you are selling. Think about the people who support you – your co-workers and family. They have needs too, and will be more receptive to helping you if you are interested in making their lives better first.

Who Is Your Customer?

First of all, I say YOU are the customer. You are the one who will spend the most time with your company, so make choices that work for you as well as for everyone else.

Some of your other customers:

Stakeholders
Investors
Existing customers
Potential customers
Suppliers
Regulatory agencies
Co-workers
Competitors

Your husband or wife
Your kids

Your body, your health …
Your conscience … your happiness … your values

What Is Your Customer's Goal?

Take a moment to think about what each of your customers want. Refer to the Feelings and Needs charts (page 121) to help you guess what specific customers may want.

After you have exercised your brain for awhile, check out your assumptions. Ask your customers what they need! Have a conversation! If you've guessed wrong, they'll correct you. They may correct you with gusto, but don't necessarily misinterpret this as meaning they're unhappy. Usually they are so thrilled that someone is finally listening to them that their excitement bubbles over with a lot of energy!

If they are unhappy or even angry and you're feeling safe enough, listen to them with sincere interest and compassion. If you can hear them out without being defensive, it could be a wonderful gift for both of you. You will probably gain some unexpected and valuable insight that will help propel your success with them and other customers. A truly honest conversation may even help you become clearer on your own personal goals. You may also possibly make a new friend.

Remember everyone is an individual and will respond best to you when you approach them accordingly.

Chapter 7: Step 2: Customers

♪

"You cannot help people who do not want to be helped."

Marshall Goldsmith
Best-selling Author
What Got You Here Won't Get You There, Succession: Are You Ready? and *MOJO: How to Get It, How to Keep It, and How to Get it Back When You Need It!*
www.MarshallGoldsmithLibrary.com

CHAPTER 8:

Business

෨

Quick Summary:

• Choose a business you enjoy, providing a needed and valued product or service to people you enjoy being with.

• Give yourself a role you can enjoy over time.

• Remember: Just because you have a product or skill does not mean the people you want to work with will buy it.

• Also: Just because you have discovered an important need and you're ready to fill it, does not mean your target market will buy it, even if they acknowledge the need.

Exercise:

1) Spend time with people you enjoy, doing activities you enjoy. While you're doing this, listen for clues about services or products they value and don't have, or needs that aren't being fulfilled. Take notes.

2) Look at your list and take some time to consider what your favorite people need and want that you could provide.

3) Put together some ideas and talk with some of your prospects about them. Get their involvement and buy-in. If they think it's a bad idea, ask other people. If they think it's a great idea, ask if they know anyone else who might be interested.

4) Test by having an entry-level offering to sell that doesn't cost you very much to provide, and gives your customer an experience of your product or service. Then you can see how committed they are to actually buying the solution they said was so valuable to them.

STEP 3: YOUR BUSINESS

Seek out and listen to feedback about you and your business.

You may have the greatest product ever, but if the timing is not right nobody will buy. In this case you must either sign up to create a new market niche, or consider adjusting your goals to fit your customers. This does not mean there is anything wrong with your pet project. It's just about being realistic with current trends.

Regardless of who you are and what you bring to the marketplace, I suggest you actively seek input from others. You could save yourself significant time and money over the long term. Once you are better acquainted with what makes you happy and what your customers need, consider adapting your business model to match your market.

Keep your original ideas on file. I find my first ideas are often inspired and it's helpful to remember what they were when the right time finally does come around.

Don't expect yourself to be good at everything. Find strategies or other people to help you with the necessary tasks you don't do as well. If the task isn't necessary, take it off your list.

Your Business Identity

Do you know what business you are in?
Do you know why?

Have you thought about how well the design of your business matches how you like to spend your day, and the way you like to work?

Most of the time the work I do feels like fun to me. I work out of my home office, and I'm responsible to my clients for the specific projects I've agreed to do for them. It's usually something I'd like to do anyway, and I enjoy the people I surround myself with. I know it's work and I know I'm in business for myself, but I often don't notice because I just wake up in the morning and start doing things I enjoy doing.

In 1987 I opened a business in a retail setting. I had a storefront with office hours. People came to my office in the morning and expected me to be there when my sign said my office opened. If there was no work to do, I stayed in the office anyway because if a customer came through the door, they needed to find me behind my desk waiting for them. If a customer came in at the end of the day and needed something first thing the next morning, I'd probably stay late and complete the work, even if I'd spent most of the day waiting for customers that didn't show up … actually, *especially* if there were no other customers that day, because I needed the revenue!

That experience helped me learn some things about myself. First of all, I was very bored waiting in my office. I realized I liked more flexibility than a retail storefront would allow. Second, it was more difficult to choose my customers based on who I enjoyed spending time with, and the work I enjoyed doing. It was a good learning experience, I made adjustments and now I'm happier in my business.

However, the retail storefront was a step closer to my heart than the job I've held just previously at a large corporation in Minnesota. I left Minnesota one winter in January. I was so done with winter that I left in a blizzard and just kept driving south until I got to Texas. Gradually I made my way to southern California, where I set up the retail storefront in a small beach town. I could see the ocean from my desk. The beach was about two blocks away, so I'd walk there during lunch.

One day during lunch at my Minnesota corporate job I told a co-worker that I was thinking of moving to California. She immediately said, "You can't do that!" It wasn't that she would miss me; it was that our culture said our place was there in the snow to suffer like everyone else, and who was I to think I was better than they were? I don't think I'm better than anyone else, but I did

Chapter 8: Step 3: Business

bring my nameplate from my corporate desk job and put it on my desk across the street from the beach. It turns out I *could* do that!

CHAPTER 9:

Focus

⁂

Quick Summary:

• Keeping the administrative side of your business running smoothly is very important.

• If this isn't your forte, find someone who is good at this to help you.

• If this is your forte, monitor yourself so you don't spend all of your time tracking no activity – be sure the sales function and other needs of your business get as much of your attention as the details.

• Be sure you keep track of promises you make, and schedule a time you'll follow through as promised.

Exercise:

1) Make a list of everything you keep track of in a spreadsheet program.

2) Add a column to the left, and label it "category". Add a category to each line.

3) Add a new column to the left, and label it "activity". For each item, type 'email', 'phone', 'visit', 'research', etc.

4) Add another column immediately to the left of the large item description column. Label this one 'priority', and assign a priority to each line item. You can use A, B, C, and A1, B3, even Z for those you decide don't need to be on the list right now, or if they are already completed and you want to keep them on the list.

5) You can now sort this list by priority, activity, and category. Add other columns as needed.

6) Make a backup copy, and use it as a working document, making changes as you think of new items, as priorities change, and as you check things off.

Step 4: Focus is Vital

Focus on tasks that are most important.

How well do you keep track of your time and resources? Do you know how you spend each hour? Or do you begin each day running and reacting and just keep going until there is no day left and you are exhausted?

Are you spending most of your time on your most important tasks? Create a list every night of the next day's most important tasks or priorities. Include both personal and business goals. If the list is too long, make it shorter or circle the one or two items that will make the most difference. Think about what is urgent, and what is important. Give more time to what's important.

Then schedule 20 minutes to one hour of quiet, uninterrupted time at the beginning of the day to focus on just those few items. Do not multi-task during this hour. Just make progress on your most important items.

Do this every day, the same time each day. Let people know which part of your day you are available, and which part of the day your door is closed and your phone unanswered. You can create a system in case there is an emergency during that hour, but usually the world can adjust and allow an hour for concentrated, focused work.

What's involved in running a business, and how do you keep track of all the details?

Which elements can you delegate to someone else, and which functions are best carried out by you personally?

How do you decide how to allocate your precious resources?

We can start with a focusing strategy familiar to all of us.

Leveraging Intention

In January are you like most people, thinking about your New Year's resolutions? And are you like most people … by December has even the memory of what your January resolutions were faded?

I make no judgments here. Anytime you take a moment to look at your life and consider what to do in the future, it's a major win.

It's too easy to keep moving through life, doing the same thing day after day, using well-worn strategies to avoid the pain of familiar things not working, and letting the years pass as we all grow older. Life is hard enough without stirring things up and making changes. Or so it seems.

We do grow older. Kids learn from what we do more than what we say, so if we're meeting our problems with angry outbursts, drugs or alcohol, or distancing ourselves from the world, so will they. If we have given up on our dreams, they will not know how to find their own. If we settle for an uninspired life within the confines of what our early conditioning allowed us to explore, the world will never benefit from our true inner gifts, and we will always know we missed the part of life that could have been the most satisfying.

But it's hard to shake things up. Our schedules are already overflowing. We are already behind in so many important projects. Why add one more thing to the list?

First of all, there are ways to create new habits that don't take a lot of time, and that can have tremendous payoffs.

Second, it's worth it to trade in a well-honed habit that takes you somewhere unsatisfying for a new habit that takes you somewhere more fun.

So if I have the intention of making some improvement in my life, how do I get from January's resolutions to December's results? Incorporate Marshall's advice into your thinking:

Chapter 9: Step 4: Focus

> "What am I willing to change now? Not in a few months. Not when I get caught up. Now. Then get started on the activity within two weeks, or take it off the list. And quit tormenting yourself!"

Marshall Goldsmith

Leverage those intentions by creating some simple accountability that will help you stay focused on your goal. The purpose … to help you remember to make a different choice when your old habit is ready to pull you into old results, and to give you a measurement in December so you can see your new results! Read about Peer Coaching and Daily Questions in the full version of this book.

♪

"As a business owner, you are the single most important factor in your business. You are the only asset you have in the beginning. You are the bank account, sales staff, worker bee—you are it.'

'If you use yourself up, there is nothing left to run your business. It's essential you learn how to balance yourself, put support systems in place, and learn to get enough energy in your day to get through it.'

'Most sole proprietors just throw themselves into the work and neglect themselves. They don't realize they have to take care of themselves first. It's like the oxygen masks on the airlines ... you have to put yours on first, because you have to survive for the business to survive.'

'This would include learning what your strengths are and accepting them. Don't fight it. Your strengths are what will make your business great. Think about who you can have come alongside you to fill in your gaps.'

'I've seen people waiting for what I call 'assistant nirvana'. They think they either have to afford a full time assistant or do it themselves. I'm a fan of 'don't spend money you don't have', but there are so many other options than spending your important time on details. You kind of have to cobble it together for awhile ... an intern two hours/day after school who can file, organize client lists on your computer ... a stay at home mom who makes calls for you ... a professional organizer two hours/month ... a way to move something forward that will give you a little more stability, a little more structure, so you can win at something else.

Cynthia Jurado
Business Coach
www.arcleadershipdynamics.com

♪

"The two essentials on everyone's to-do list are exercise and hobbies. We have to stop viewing these as indulgent luxuries. Exercise is one of the best tools we can use to take care of ourselves so we can operate efficiently. Physical activity relates directly to self-esteem because we feel confident when we look and feel good. Our self-worth increases and we feel more powerful when we can do more because we have more energy."

Saundra Pelletier
Speaker and author of *Saddle Up Your Own White Horse*
www.SaundraPelletier.com

CHAPTER 10:
Sales

෨෮

Quick Summary:

• For any business to be successful, someone has to sell something.

• If this isn't your forte, find someone who is good at this to help you.

• If this is your forte, make sure you are keeping track of the promises you make, and find someone to help you with the details.

• If you feel shy about promoting yourself, focus instead on the message.

• Make only commitments you can keep.

• Have a professional business card.

Exercise:

1) Look at your promotional materials and messages in various mediums. Are they consistent? Are the claims accurate? Are you using benefit statements? Do they address the needs of your target audience? Do they look and sound attractive and compelling to your target audience?

2) Really listen to your customers. Find out how they heard about you. Do more of that.

3) Ask your happy customers for referrals.

Step 5: Someone has to sell

Sell your personal brand along with your product.

For any business to be successful, someone has to sell something. If you're managing your career, you are selling your personal brand. If you're shy, join Toastmasters or get involved with a professional group. Practice talking with people. Think about what you have to offer professionally, and learn to convey this in brief statements people will respond to with interest.

How likeable are you? Do people trust you? Read *What Got You Here Won't Get You There* by Marshall Goldsmith and see if you can discover ways to become more effective in your interactions.

Do you like to sell, or hate to sell?
Be honest about it, and be sure you are always doing something to promote your business. I've found it takes about two years of promotion until new business starts coming in by itself, and consistent promotion makes a big difference.

Marshall Goldsmith is one of the most successful individual entrepreneurs I know. He is one coach, and his business activities all revolve around him being a coach. Yet he has a very successful international business, and his name has become a recognizable brand worldwide. How did he do this?

Well, aside from his eight million+ frequent flier miles, his endless energy meeting with clients, speaking to thousands of people in audiences throughout the world, and having written over 20 books, he is continually promoting himself and his work. When I met him in 2002 his schedule was full and he had an 8-month waiting list for coaching clients. Someone asked him why he kept promoting his services when he was already so successful. His answer, "My calendar is full *because* I continue to promote my work."

Where do your customers come from? Referrals are the best source. Who do your happy customers know that could use your services, and would they mind introducing you to them?

There are many ways to get the word out.

When you're in business for yourself, your business associates are the network of professionals who help you develop and maintain your business, your customers, and your potential customers … in short, everyone.

Do you have a presentation ready that demonstrates the value potential customers will receive, describes your products and services clearly, and gives the listener a clear next step to begin working with you? What can you say in

15 seconds on an elevator, and what can you say in a one-hour sales presentation? Be prepared for either, and anything in between.

On Paper

Start by creating a flier. The following will help you think through what you want to say. Later you can adapt your printed message to other mediums. Make sure you create a professional business card you feel proud to hand people you meet.

Sheryl Roush, an experienced graphic designer and speaker, asked me to share the following with you:

> **Marketing Your Services in Print:**
> **3 Stages for Designing an**
> **Effective Flyer**
>
> You are talented, have great expertise, and offer a valuable service to others. How do you get their attention and generate a response?
>
> When creating any promotion, begin by placing yourself in your potential BUYER'S shoes, think like THEY think. Become your buyer. A big mistake in most

promotional pieces is that they are designed from the SELLER'S point-of-view. What is their "pain" and how is your service the "solution?"

There are three stages of rapport required in any promotion: 1) Relevance; 2) Confirmation; and 3) Action. These stages must be done in order for your promotion to be effective.

Stage 1. In the first 1-7 seconds the buyer is looking for the relevance of your service, the benefits, or "WIIFM?" Placed in the top one-third of your layout, the reader browses short body copy, graphics, images, and color. Name their pain in the form of a question to compel them to read further. Since 70-80% of readers are "skimmers" and quick decision makers, use subheads and bullets for this group.

Stage 2 is up to 90 seconds, where your reader is still trying to decide whether this is a "match" for them, or not. Avid readers continue reading the piece and require longer body text plus all the facts and details to make a well-informed decision. Consider adding testimonials from satisfied buyers. This stage utilizes the middle portion of the layout and toward the bottom of the layout.

Stage 3 is vital in your promotion. Based on how engaged your buyer is and how well you have addressed their needs in the first two stages, the reader will naturally "flow" into this bottom one-third of the layout. This is the Call to Action stage, where you instruct the reader how to respond affirmatively to what they have read. This is the best place for your logo, email, toll free phone number, website. Create a "sense of urgency" using bold italics (i.e., Call today for your free 15-minute consultation!).

After you finish your draft, show it to others, ideally in your target market. How easily do they follow it? Is it compelling enough for them to take action? What is missing? What can be removed? Is it buyer-centered? Minimize the use of "we" and "our" and maximize "your" and "you" in the copy and headlines.

To generate higher response, use all three stages in any promotion you create!

Sheryl Roush, International Trainer on Marketing Design and Author of ***Solid Gold Newsletter Design***
www.SparklePresentations.com

Online

I've been working with the Internet and online marketing since 1996. Things have changed a bit since then, and I expect they will change more by the time you're reading this book. If I explain something technical to you right now, some element of what I'm explaining will probably change by the time I've finished writing the sentence.

So I won't go into anything technical. There are some principles I've learned that stood me well in the 90s that still hold up today, and I expect these principles will continue to be useful in the future. I will keep more updated information on my website, www.CoachMarilyn.com. You can also check out my book Social Media for Small Business: Tips on Using Your Time Effectively. Here are some ways to think about your online promotion:

1) Don't put anything online that you would not want said about you in front of your boss, your co-workers, your spouse, your children. Honesty and integrity count here, too. One world flows into another, as people who search on your name or business name will find everything that is out there about you. It's a lot like a small town.

2) Be careful about playing technical tricks with the search engines. Some strategies are useful because they help search engines determine the topic of your content. Other strategies can get you black-listed. Strategies like putting thousands of keywords in colored text the same color as the page background color were out of date by 1999. Don't do that. Just try to play it straight, and use title tags, header tags, and meta tags to describe the actual content on your web page. Make the content easy to read, and filled with valuable information for the reader. Use key words

throughout the content, in context. When you create a link, make sure the words you are linking go to a page with content that is congruent with the words in the link. And so on. Congruence between what you say the page is about and the actual content on the page is important. That's the magic here.

3) Don't misuse email lists to spam, and don't abuse the hospitality of networking and discussion sites to sell yourself in a way that offends the members. Get to know the members honestly, find out what they need, and offer a solution if you have one. Just like the real world. Be respectful, polite, and make real connections with like-minded people. The rest will follow.

4) Your online promotion probably will not replace your other forms of promotion, but simply enhance and augment them. Putting your website url on your printed material allows people to follow up at their convenience in a non-threatening way as they look over what you've put on your website. If they find this reassuring, or they find what they are looking for, they may give you a call or stop by, or take the next step in the call to action on your website.

In Person

As head of your organization, you are your organization's image and reputation. What do your business associates see about your business when they interact with you? How do they feel about coming back to you and your company? This is your best and most powerful advertising. Learn how to handle some of the tough situations that can come your way.

Preparing a presentation:

- What is your purpose?

- Who is the audience?

- Outline key points in simple language.

- Practice, practice, practice.

- Copy any handouts.

- Practice in the meeting room if possible.

- Get there early.

Chapter 10: Step 5: Sales

Questions to ask yourself when preparing your presentation:

1) Credibility: What gives me the right to talk about this?

2) What can I say in the first 60 seconds to get their attention?

3) What are some stories to illustrate my points?

4) What do I want the audience to do or feel at the end of my presentation?

(Notes from **Dave Almos'** course "Innovation in Business" San Diego 2008)

♪

"What suggestions do I have for someone starting a new business? Do your homework! Then try a couple of things, and finally put your resources into what works."

Jess Serrano
Co-Owner, Studio 69 Hair Salon
San Diego, CA

CHAPTER 11:

Follow-up & Delivery

Quick Summary:

• Be curious about how your customers perceive their experience with you and your company and products, and ask for their valuable feedback.

• Be ready to make changes to show your customers that you are sincere about your desire to improve.

• If you can't make the improvement, tell your customers why, and let them know you value their business.

Chapter 11: Step 6: Follow-up & Delivery

Exercise:

1) Ask your customers about their experience with you. Tell them you would like to improve, and ask if they have any suggestions.

2) Remember to just listen without any judgment or hurt feelings. Keep in mind, you are sincerely interested, and the only way to find out is to ask. Take notes.

3) Thank them for their candor and willingness to share.

STEP 6: FOLLOW-UP & DELIVERY

Ask how you are doing and deliver on your promises.

Now you have your customers, you have your business and your product or service. How are you doing on the delivery side?

Are you clear about what you have promised your customers?

Are you there when they look for you?

What can you do to improve your business in your customers' eyes?

Resist the urge to just keep going along the same track without asking your customers how you're doing. Why not ask? People like being asked for their opinion. It conveys respect and appreciation, which is what you want your customers to feel when they think of you.

There is so much valuable information to be gained by asking. Whether what your customers say is accurate or inaccurate, remember that you are listening for their perception and they are the ones writing the check.

Even if they have a negative perception, you need to know what they are thinking. If you ask the question, they can let you know the problem, and you have a chance to fix it. If you can't fix it, you can at least let them know how much you value the relationship.

Feedback

How do we know who we are in the world?

We can see in the eyes of the people around us how they view us ... if we're paying attention.

Most of us don't relish the idea of 'feedback' ... we have had too much experience with what sounded like criticism, judgment, analysis. We have responded with longwinded explanations which not only went unappreciated, but seemed to actually fuel distance between us and our intended message, and our desired connection and rapport with the other person.

Read about Feed*Forward* in the full version of this book.

You Can Fire a Customer

I used to think only employees could be fired, and I used to think a customer could choose not to do business with me, but that I didn't have the same right to choose not to work with a particular customer. I've found it's very important to both me and my customers that I'm honest about whether or not the relationship is working out.

There may be some legal considerations depending upon your industry. I will leave that up to you and your attorney. I'm just going to talk about the personal management side of things.

You may know it's time for you as the leader to step in and do something about a customer that is not working out. This is not your favorite thing. Where do you start?

I say first take your time to get real clear with yourself. What is it that you really need and want from that person or role right now? Try to go a little deeper with your own understanding of yourself, because that will help you get what you need in the process. Make a list of specific behaviors and requests so the person knows exactly what you want from them, and where things are not going so well from your perspective.

Go into this with an open heart and be willing to learn something new from this offending customer you are probably pretty frustrated with by now. Acknowledge your feelings to yourself and leave them and your judgments at the door so you can have an honest conversation with this person.

Listen with sincere interest as the other person (if they feel safe enough with you), reveals what is going on for them. If the words you hear push your buttons, take a deep breath and remember it's not about you; they are just expressing their needs in the best way their skills allow. They are just talking about themselves. If you're interested in developing the relationship, why not be interested in what is unique about this person?

Then decide together your next step. Consider being creative. You are the captain steering the boat; allow them to inform your decision because respect and trust can build long-term commitment, or perhaps an advocate if parting is the best course.

Do we really need more enemies in our lives? I prefer to create more friends.

♫

"You become the star when you listen, because listening validates the other person."

Oprah Winfrey
Media Mogul and Philanthropist
"Oprah" Television Show 2008
www.Oprah.com

CHAPTER 12:
Review & Celebrate
℘

Quick Summary:

• The business world is constantly changing. Be willing to adjust your business model accordingly without undermining what is currently successful for you.

• Life and business are easier when you're having fun. Take time to celebrate, both at the end of a project, and all throughout the process.

• Thank the people who have helped you.

Chapter 12: Step 7: Review & Celebrate

Exercise:

1) Stay on top of market changes in your industry.

2) Constantly ask yourself if this affects your business, or if it could in the future.

3) Make notes about possible strategies that you can refer to as needed in the future.

4) Make changes if needed.

5) Make sure you have at least some fun every day, so you stay lighthearted and inspired.

6) Think about your customers and do something to add fun, pleasure or appreciation to their day.

Step 7: Review & Celebrate

Review your business so far, celebrate and have some fun.

Life and business are easier when you are having fun. People are more attracted to you when you are light-hearted and inspired. Remember what makes you happy, and include it as part of your day. Think about what makes your customers happy, and spend part of your day doing something fun for them you know they will appreciate. That little extra really makes a difference.

Recalibrate: Alignment with Goals
Remember your original vision, before life got so complicated with new business, new issues, new opportunities?

How are you doing in terms of following your original plan? As a matter of fact, does your original plan still fit the marketplace, and have you learned anything new about how you really want to spend your day?

Does anything need to be updated? How will you make edits to your original plan without losing important ground?

Chris Coffey offered the following for this book. This is the review process he uses with his coaching clients:

After Action Review:
What did you set out to do?
Why?
What actually happened?
Why did it happen?
What insights did you have?
What are you going to do moving forward?

Chris Coffey
Keynote Speaker, Leadership Coach and Trainer
www.ChristopherCoffey.com

Our economic world is changing very rapidly. It's imperative to keep checking back with our own personal business assumptions regularly, and be prepared to adjust our business choices as our market and our business environment change.

Pitfalls to Avoid
I asked David G. Thomson, author of Blueprint to a Billion, what characteristics help a leader grow their business from startup to $50 million.

"A leader would need to be a fast worker, a fast problem solver, able to build a team dynamically, and able to share leadership for their idea with their team. You have to find your other half, and give that person actual power" (see inside/outside leadership in Blueprint to a Billion).'

'In my research I found the odds of failure were greater than the odds of success, and I discovered three common pitfalls:

First Pitfall: Beware the founder or inventor who has an idea they cannot explain in terms customers and investors can understand.

Second Pitfall: Beware the founding or engineering team that believes their own hype.

Third Pitfall: Get people in the boat who are really on board.'

'I found the people with the most passion tended to go out of business, because they never knew when to let go of an idea that was not working. It is like walking through a maze. You do come to dead ends when you walk through a maze, and you have to be wise enough to turn around rather than continuing to hit your head against the wall.'

'In terms of leadership, you have to be flexible, and you want to be passionate, but it is important to be passionate and have goals toward the direction of the idea rather than the specific idea. You start your business with a specific model in mind. Your initial model will evolve based on what you learn along the way. You have to be flexible enough to reshape your idea as you listen to customers, so you deliver something that is highly valued.'

'As a leader, you have to be flexible, humble, and a good listener. You want to have a balance between passion and pragmatism or reality. You want to have good problem solving skills, and you want to have integrity.'

'When you do not have that foundation, you may start to grow a company, but invariably you fail. You have to be consistent about this while you go from one million to one billion. It is about being consistent over a long time frame in a consistent way with a consistent set of values."

David G. Thomson
Author, *Blueprint to a Billion*
Business Advisor to Growth Companies
www.BlueprintGrowth.com

Celebrate
You have been dreaming big and working hard.

You have stretched and found new ways to accomplish goals you were not so sure you could achieve.

It's time to take a moment to enjoy the benefits of your labor.

Is everything perfect?

Chapter 12: Step 7: Review & Celebrate

Have you accomplished everything according to plan?

Are you everything you would like to be?

Probably not!

That is part of the process. Celebrate the mystery too, because you have probably gained some real treasures that were not on your list either.

Take a moment and rest. Thank everyone who has helped you.

Especially yourself.

Give yourself a day off and spend it exactly the way you want.

♪

"I believe if you do anything with passion, there is a success behind it."

Marie Osmond on The Larry King Show 2008

TOOLS & RESOURCES

Personal Management Tools to Help You Focus

Daily Routine

I'd like you to come up with your own personal daily routine that supports your way of doing things. In the meantime, you can borrow mine, which I outline below. Even if you don't have time to do anything else toward your new goals today, at least take five minutes in the morning and five minutes at night to try this:

Morning

• Before getting out of bed, take a moment to welcome the new day.

• Remember your vision, and take a moment to see and feel how it will be when you are living the successful outcome of your vision.

• Thank (God, the Universe, your Higher Self, as you choose) for the wonderful people who will touch your life today, and ask that your interaction with everyone be a blessing to them and to you.

• Thank (God, the Universe, your Higher Self, as you choose) for the successful outcome of your goals today, and become open to learning something new through unexpected opportunities that bring you even closer to your highest good.

• As you wake up, look at your list of things to do, and imagine everything going smoothly and easily to get you closer to your vision.

Evening
Just before going to sleep:

• Say this to yourself (attributed to Ralph Waldo Emerson): "Finish each day and be done with it. You have done what you could. Some blunders and absurdities no doubt crept in; forget them as soon as you can. Tomorrow is a new day; begin it well and serenely."

• Let go of any lingering feeling of discomfort in mind, body or spirit, and go to sleep with a feeling of gratitude, focusing your imagination on what you want.

I know that going from a feeling of stress or argument to manufacturing a feeling of gratitude may seem farfetched, but I recommend you cultivate this ability. You don't have to be grateful for the way things are, but I have found real magic in being grateful in the midst of the mess. You are in the middle of something you don't like and apparently can't get out of in the moment anyway, so why not do what you can about it … change your attitude and at least become more comfortable. I'm not exaggerating when I say that I have had amazingly positive experiences using this technique in situations that from the outside looked certain to be unhappy.

Your To Do List
Now, what do you put on your list of things to do today?

1. Mind Dump & Says Who
I know you have many obligations to many others, including family, job, maintaining your residence, taking care of yourself. You probably don't even remember all of the things you do. Do a mind-dump. Write them all down. If you can, list them in a spreadsheet, and in the column to the left of the list of items, put the name of the person or organization you are doing this for. If you are sure you are doing something just for yourself, then put your own name down.

2. Now Do a Best-Case Scenario
Pretend you have all the time, health, money and opportunity in the world and make a list of all the things you really want to do. Everything you can think of, from eating ice cream for dinner to

taking a cruise around the world. You don't have to do everything on your list. It does feel good to honor yourself enough to acknowledge your desires and put those on the list along with taking out the garbage and making your bed.

3. Vision

Does every item on your list have a person or organization or goal in the column to the left of it? Create another column on the left and think again about your vision that gets your juices going every morning. Put a number or a word in that column for each item indicating how closely that task aligns with your vision. This is more of a feeling exercise than an intellectual exercise, because your filters are probably geared more toward what you've always done in the past than what is possible in the future. You can always go back and change things later. For now just take your first gut reaction.

4. Priority

You knew this was coming. Make one more column to the left and put a priority on each one: A is most important, D least important, and Z something you don't want to even think about for now. You can add A1, A2, D3, etc., whatever makes sense to you. Create a key if it helps you remember later what you had in mind.

What it Means

This all just gives you good food for thought. In a spreadsheet you can sort by any column.

Sort by the "Priority" column and then look at the "Vision" and "Says Who" columns. Are some people or organizations in your life already more closely aligned with your vision?

Just take some time to look over your list from different points of view, and see what you can learn about yourself and your life.

You might feel very motivated and ready to make a big personal improvement list. I'll be happy if you just choose one or two things to improve. Again, here is what Marshall Goldsmith tells his clients to ask themselves:

> "What am I willing to change now? Not in a few months. Not when I get caught up. Now. Then get started on the activity within two weeks, or take it off the list. And quit tormenting yourself!"

Marshall Goldsmith

Environment

What is the quality of your environments, and how well do they support you? Depending on the facet of your life or business you are focusing on, several environments may come into play. Use this random list of environments to help you plan projects, set goals, identify needs and resources:

Money
Strategic network

Physical location
Physical body and health

Relationships, family, social
Friends: male and female

Self image, self concept
Quiet time with self
Spiritual, nature

Learning, exploration, intellectual
emotional freedom and support

Community
Play, leisure

Section Four: Personal Management Tools

Financial Tips

Consult your CPA or financial advisor for specifics which relate to your industry.

The basics are simple:

1. Earn more than you spend.
2. Save what you can.
3. Use a budget.

If you're thinking about going into business, I recommend starting as lean as possible. Do you really have to lease that fancy office space and hire a full time receptionist? What can you do with no overhead at all? Can you start by just cultivating relationships with prospective customers and providing a service which costs little but your time?

Can you start by trying out different ideas while still enjoying a stabilizing income from your current source of revenue? Unless you have no other source of income and this is your only option, giving up your current source of security may be unnecessarily putting yourself at the edge of terror. Building a business takes confidence and focus. This is not the time to increase unnecessary challenges.

When asked to define a successful Amway business, Jay Van Andel, co-founder of Amway, is reported to say, "One that is profitable."

In a conversation between John Travolta and Larry King on The Larry King Show in 2008, John Travolta said he uses a budget. When Larry asked him, "Even you?" John replied, "If you want to keep any money, you have to budget. Anybody could lose what they make if they don't budget."

For more information:

Your Money or Your Life: Transforming Your Relationship with Money and Achieving Financial Independence by Vicki Robin, Joe Dominguez, and Monique Tilford
Penguin   ISBN 978-0143115762

Section Four: Personal Management Tools

Finding Your Desk

How important is organization? I've been coaching small business owners for years on organizational principles from keeping track of those floating pieces of paper with phone numbers and appointments on them, to filing systems that work for both actuaries and sales people and procedures to streamline the paper flow in a business.

You might think that means my own office is spotless, with everything in its place. Although that is something I would enjoy, I also value the creative process, which can get very messy. To quote my friend David Lober: "What comes out of a workshop is more important than the condition of the workshop."

When paper comes in, I have one pile for important information I need to keep over time, a pile for things to do in the near future, and another pile for things I want to keep but don't have time to file yet. When it takes me longer to find a piece of paper than it should, that is when I know it's worth taking time to organize the pile.

Not everyone can think in a messy or chaotic environment. Not everyone can think in a spotless, sterile environment. Know what works for you, and create an environment that supports you and your process.

In case you are ready to create a filing system for your home office, here is a basic outline to start with:

Information (A-Z storage files)

1) Take 26 file folders (I get third cut without reinforced tabs, because I go through a lot of file folders.

2) Write a letter from A – Z on each folder tab.

3) Put them in a file drawer or box.

4) Keep some blank file folders nearby.

5) When you bring home some papers you want to keep for awhile, label a blank file folder, put the papers in the folder, and place the folder in alphabetical order. Simple.

6) Once a year or so, go through the folders to see if there is anything you can throw away or file in last year's archive.

Categorize

Here are some general categories you could use:

Personal
- Car
- Finances
- Health
- House
- School
- Shopping (this can help you save time and gas on errands)

Business
- Accounting
- Brochures
- Contacts
- Customers
- Events
- Goals
- Resource Material

Action Items (Hot Files)
- Bills to Pay
- Correspondence to Do
- Orders to Fill
- People to Call
- Read (keep this small unless you have a lot of time to read)

- Tickle (holding for more information, future events, etc.)
- To Do This Week (review this once a week)

Focus Session

What do very successful people report most often as their secret to success? "Focus!"

Before I go to bed at night, and after I wake up in the morning, I do a Focus Session with myself.

• I sit down in a quiet place with my planner and look at my values and goals, and allow myself to feel what I will experience when I actually achieve those goals.

• Then I look at what I have planned for the upcoming day, and see how closely they are aligned with my values and overall goals.

• Is everything I'm planning to do actually addressing my needs, or have I taken on responsibilities that are not mine?

• What can I add to my day to inspire me and keep me happy?

• All of this takes about five minutes. I do this again throughout the day as I have time.

Healthy Exercises

If you consider there's only one of you, and your income and business rely on your ability to perform, hopefully you'll be motivated to give premium attention to your most important physical asset: your body.

I have often wondered why something so important has become a chore rather than a pleasure. Maybe it goes back to our teenage years when it was cool to smoke, drink, drive fast cars and try risky sexual exploits. It was not cool to take good care of ourselves, eat healthy food, floss our teeth, and maintain the clear head we needed to manage an already challenging transition in our lives. For those lucky enough to survive reckless experimentation without lifelong addictions or crippling disabilities, we still seem to carry habits we might do better without.

Personally I'm changing my own internal paradigms as I become aware of bad habits of thought and action, to paradigms and habits that support my health and make better use of my resources. Following is a list of new habits I've collected that might be helpful to you:

Morning

• Brush and floss teeth (did you know gum disease has been linked to heart issues, and that flossing even occasionally can help prevent gum disease?)

• Lie on the floor and do some exercises to start the day to help brain and body work together.

• Eat a healthy breakfast with protein within an hour of waking up.

• Take food supplements as needed to get complete nutrition for the day.

During the Day

• Walk, go up and down stairs, park on the far side of the parking lot, take every opportunity to get exercise.

• When reading or at the computer where eyes are at a fixed distance for long periods of time, get up at least every half hour and walk around. Look up at least every ten minutes and look at varying distances closer and farther away than the fixed computer or reading distance.

- When picking up something heavy, either get help, or use legs to lift rather than back to bear the weight. If possible, take it apart and move it in pieces, one piece at a time.

- Go to the gym as possible and follow a regular exercise plan to improve strength, flexibility and endurance.

- Drink plenty of water.

- Eat a healthy lunch that contains protein.

Before Going to Bed

- Make a list or journal or sort out anything stressful before going to sleep, so it doesn't affect resting time.

- Avoid eating two to three hours before going to bed.

- Turn off the TV and listen to some soothing music and read something uplifting and positive before turning off the light.

When Traveling

• Drink plenty of water.

• Have clothes and accessories that match the climate and weather.

• Bring healthy snacks, including protein snacks.

• Take extra food supplements as needed.

• Do Feldenkrais exercises when sitting for long periods of time.

When Stressed

• Take a deep, silent, conscious loving breath.

• Focus on what I want, instead of any bothersome thoughts.

I asked Arthur Joseph's advice one difficult period in my life when a series of losses finally penetrated my 'I can get through this' veneer. Feelings were beginning to surge over the levee, and I needed a way to focus. Arthur became quiet for a moment, and then suggested I try focusing on allowing a conscious loving breath.

This sounded very simple. I could remember the instructions. He did not say 'take' a deep breath, he said 'allow a conscious loving breath'. This took a little practice, especially when I was busy trying to hold back my feelings ... from whom? Mostly from myself. The breath took me through the levees I'd built up to and through the feelings, I started to relax, and life began to look reasonable again, despite current circumstances.

Taking Exercise to the Next Level

One of the healthiest exercises I know is called 'gratitude'. That may sound schlocky and pollyannaish, but I've found it to be very powerful, especially in situations least suited to gratitude. I've learned I don't have to practice being grateful for the situation I'm in to get the benefits, but just by being grateful in the situation.

Several years ago I was dating a man with children whose ex-wife was very much still in the picture. One day I found myself driving to the ex-wife's mother's home to meet with his ex-wife and her mother ... by myself. As I drove, I wondered how in the world I had gotten myself into this situation. I had no idea how this was going to go, but I definitely knew I was outnumbered and going into 'enemy' territory.

I remembered the concept of practicing gratitude. I started choosing to feel gratitude ... within myself, not for anything specific, just to feel gratitude as I was going through the experience. Somehow the visit went very well, and we all ended up leaving our time together feeling good. Who would have thought?! Afterward I could authentically practice gratitude for the situation as I drove home!!

If a healthy attitude helps our bodies become more healthy physically, then practicing gratitude seems a good choice!

For more information:

Relaxercise by David and Kaethe Zemach-Bersin, and Mark Reese
HarperCollins ISBN 0-06-250992-6

Vocal Power by Arthur Samuel Joseph
Vocal Awareness Institute ISBN 978-1-588-72064-1

How to Use a Planner

I'm used to the Franklin-Covey planner, so I'll make suggestions that work with their system. If you use another system, just add sections to your planner to get the function. If you only use an electronic planner, find ways to incorporate these functions into your system, either electronically or on paper you carry with you.

When I'm spending most of my time in my home office, I can keep track of my appointments on my computer, and sync with my PDA to carry with me. When I go out, I add new appointments to my PDA and sync with my computer.

When I'm spending most of my time out of the office, meeting new people and attending meetings, I use my paper planner as well. It's just easier for me to take notes with pen and paper than to power up my PDA, find the right place and type one character at a time when I get a new phone number or information I want to remember. I keep this as auxiliary information, and when I get back to the office at the end of the day I review my notes and add them to my computer or PDA as appropriate, and then sync the PDA and computer.

Section Four: Personal Management Tools

Life used to be easier! If you don't need to keep track of certain details, don't worry about it. Organizational tools are there to make your life easier by helping you keep track of details that help you be more productive. If the planner is asking for something you don't need, just know it's there in case your circumstances change in the future. Use only the elements that help you now.

Elements (sections of your planner)

- **General**:
    o Master task list (items with no specific time frame)
    o Values & goals (see "Values-Based Time Management" 116)
    o Focus (see "Focus Session" 96)
    o Contacts
    o Notes

- **Annual**:
    o Calendar
    - this year
    - at least one year in the future
    - last year

- **Monthly:** (you may prefer weekly)
    o Index
    o Goals for this month

- **Daily**:
    - o Task list
    - o Appointment schedule
    - o Journal
    - o Expenses

Carry your planner with you everywhere. Develop a routine so you make sure you have it with you when you leave the house, your table at the restaurant, a meeting. It contains personal information like your wallet or purse, so keep track of it as you do your wallet or purse. As you go through the day, write down notes, phone numbers, and appointments all in one place … your planner.

When I meet a new person and get their business card, I write their name, phone number, email and pertinent information in the contacts section. I keep the business card and file it at home in my "Contacts" file.

If I find out there is an upcoming meeting, or an agency or person to follow up with, I turn to the journal page for today, and write it there. I give it a title which I underline: Annual Meeting, and underneath I write the details. Then I go to the monthly index page, in the first column write today's date, and in the second column write "Annual Meeting". The index is wonderful! Three months from now I'll remember I wrote the annual meeting information somewhere, and I don't have to dig through my pile of papers, or go through each daily planner page. I can just look through a few monthly index pages until I find the listing, and then turn to the right daily page to find my notes.

If I'm at a meeting and I know I'll need several pages to take notes, I start a new page in the "Notes" section of my planner, and use as many pages as I like. I can move those pages to today's daily page, and make an entry in the monthly index so I can locate the notes later. Sometimes I type the notes into my computer later, and if so, I copy them into the "Notes" section of my PDA software so I have them electronically if I need them. But then I'm a techie. You may want to keep things more paper based.

It's important to prioritize your list of daily tasks, so you don't spend your valuable time getting pulled into a long-winded conversation about an item that is not your priority, or sometimes even your responsibility. Know where you're going today, and keep yourself on track. I prioritize using A, B, C and Z. I change priorities on my computer to Z when they are complete, because when I sort they go to the bottom of the list. Not all As are equal: use A1, A2, A3 etc. to further prioritize, so you know what to start with first.

Some of your priorities you can delegate to others. Keep them at the same priority level on your planner; just make a note of who you delegated to, and when they are supposed to do what. If this gets very complicated, you might want to use project management software to keep track of specific projects with timelines and tasks that are dependent, meaning if someone is late getting back to you on their task, and other people are not able to start their part and the whole project becomes late, then you have a cascading effect on your plans for each task in the project. Let the project management software make the adjustments for you. See the "Project Management" section in the full version of this book.

That's about it. The most important thing: Keep everything in one place, or at least somewhere you can find it again. When you reach for a piece of paper to write down some important bit of information, reach for your planner and write it there where you can find it easily.

Section Four: Personal Management Tools

Needs Literacy

Our human needs play an enormous role underlying every decision we make and everything we do. Sometimes it helps to get down to basics when we're trying to understand a situation, or to solve a problem.

Needs Hierarchy

Abraham Maslow organizes human needs into essential categories, one building upon the other:

• Physiological needs must first be met to sustain life: breathing, food, water, sex, sleep, homeostasis, excretion.

• Safety needs come next: security of body, employment resources, morality, the family, health, property.

• Love and belonging needs build upon the first two: friendship, family, sexual intimacy.

• Esteem is next: self-esteem, confidence, achievement, respect of others, respect by others.

• Self-actualization can be achieved after the preceding need categories are met: morality, creativity, spontaneity, problem solving, lack of prejudice, acceptance of facts.

Universal Human Needs

The Center for Nonviolent Communication uses needs as the basis for helping people in conflict understand each other. They list the following needs as being held by everyone. For complete list, see Needs Chart (page 121).

- Social connection
- Physical well-being
- Honesty
- Play
- Peace
- Meaning
- Autonomy

Needs-Based Communication Model

As taught by the Center for Nonviolent Communication:

1. **Observation**: Simply describe what a camera would see, without editorial filters of any kind.

2. **Feelings**: Guess what feelings the person may be experiencing (see the Feelings Charts 121) Note: If they correct you, that is a step forward in getting clarity. "I feel that …" is not a feeling.

3. **Needs**: Guess what needs the person may be experiencing. Again, if they correct you, it's a positive step forward. "I need (person's name) to …" doesn't count. What needs is the person speaking experiencing? (see the Needs Chart 126)

4. **Request**: Make a clear, present request, something doable in the moment. What exactly would that person want who to do now to get closer to what they want?

Conflict Resolution

Needs identification becomes very important in any negotiation. As you become more adept at identifying needs in yourself, you will become better at guessing what need the other person is trying to get met. In a conflict, you may discover you share the same need, or you each have needs that balance each other in some way. Bringing this awareness can make conversations and negotiations go much more smoothly.

Once each party can hear the authentic needs of the other party, strategies to get everyone's needs met often become obvious and easy. Often the conflicting parties are actually trying to get the same need met, and are simply approaching it with different strategies. When this becomes clear, we stop seeing the other party as an enemy, and our desire to reach out to another human being in pain motivates us to find solutions that work for everyone.

Needs Literacy Exercise:
To practice identifying needs in yourself and others, try making these lists when you have a quiet moment:

1. How you are most likely to speak to yourself when you are less than perfect? You probably speak to others this way, too.

2. What words or phrases come to mind when you're angry with others, or when you're judging them?

3. What stimulates defensive thoughts and hurt or angry feelings in you? Notice what the other person said, or what you thought they meant.

4. What are you most afraid that others might think of you?

As you look at your list, notice what feelings come up in you, and consider which of your needs might be met or unmet.

Whose Need?

During group conversations and meetings, it's helpful to keep track of whose need is on the table. Sometimes during a discussion a person's need gets met without having to achieve the strategy or end goal they originally brought into the conversation. Sometimes through thoughtful conversation at a need level, the entire paradigm of the conversation can shift as transparent sharing begins to illuminate an entirely new level of depth to the issue being discussed.

For more information:

www.cnvc.org

Quality Cave Time

When life and work get busy and you feel pulled from all angles and don't know which way to turn … take a moment to remember your favorite thing to do, and check your calendar to see how long it's been since you gave yourself any personal time.

Sometimes even five minutes can make a difference. If you can get by yourself where nothing is required of you for five minutes, it doesn't cost much time or any money to sit quietly with your eyes closed and imagine your dream vacation … with you in the picture. Feel the sun on the beach, the cool mountain breeze, hear the wind in the sails, or the horse's gallop as you go riding. Just five minutes. We allow our bodies to experience plenty of stress as we imagine what might go wrong day to day; why not use this technique in reverse and imagine what we would like to go right!

How you get your quiet time is up to you. I just added this page to the book to remind you: You sometimes make better decisions when you're feeling fulfilled instead of depleted.

By the way, women need cave time, too!

Section Four: Personal Management Tools

Values-Based Time Management

You've probably already slept through several time management courses. So have I. Here are some ideas to help time management work for you, and hopefully be more fun.

First, make life easier by keeping track of the paper and information that comes into your life. See "How to Use a Planner" (page 103) and "Finding Your Desk" (page 92). When you can see past your desktop and locate the time of today's meeting, you are out of survival mode and can begin thinking about self-actualization.

I keep a saying on my wall, "Nothing should be more highly prized than the value of each day" by Goethe. None of us knows how much time we have left, or under what condition tomorrow will find ourselves or our environment.

Going through life unconsciously may mean looking up one day and wondering where the last 20 years went. If I've gotten up each day for 20 years and decided not to plan and just let life happen, then okay. If I've let other people decide for me what is important in my life and how I should use my time and I wake up 20 years later, that is not so okay.

Consciously managing my time is a way of taking control of my own life. Starting from awareness of my values gives me power to control the direction of my life toward what matters to me, and what makes me happy.

Identifying Values

How do I know what my values are? I asked Nathaniel Branden that question, and he gave me some sentence completion exercises. You can find his entire program in the appendix of *The Art of Living Consciously*. I suggest you use the following questions to help you develop a list of values you would like to live by over the next year:

> One of the traits I look for in people is …
> One of the rules I try to live by is …
> I respect people most when they …
> I do not respect people when they …
> Sometimes I am drawn to people who …
> Right now it seems to me that …
>
> One of the principles that guides me is …
> One of the things I want out of life is …

One of the things I want from people is …
One of the things I want from work is …
One of the things I expect of myself is …
I am becoming aware …

Life seems most fulfilling when …
Life seems most painful when …
I feel most alive when …
I am beginning to suspect …

Nathaniel Branden
The Art of Living Consciously

What to Do Next

Ranking
Now that you have your list of values, rank them in order of importance to you.

Start with your most important value. Think about how the outcome of that value could manifest in your life by this time next year. Write a description of this, and include how you feel as you experience this positive outcome of what matters most to you. Make it about you and your experience, not about someone else's life.

- When you have the description, think about when, realistically, this might actually happen.

- Now make a list of the practical steps it would take to bring this about.

- Break them down into what has to happen monthly and weekly to make this happen.

Put Them Where You Can Find Them
Pull out your planner:

- Put these goals into your planner by month and week as appropriate.

- Now think about some task you can do every day to get closer to this goal.

- Put this task, or these tasks, on your daily pages, or a master task list that you look at every day.

- Put the description you wrote in Step 1 above in the "Focus" section of your planner so you can refer to it regularly.

Looking Deeper
Do this for each of your values, in order of priority.

Section Four: Personal Management Tools

For more information:

The Art of Living Consciously by Nathaniel Branden
Simon & Schuster
ISBN: 978-0-684-81084-3

Feelings Chart

Feelings when your needs <u>are</u> satisfied:

AFFECTIONATE
compassionate
friendly
loving
open hearted
sympathetic
tender
warm

CONFIDENT
empowered
open
proud
safe
secure

ENGAGED
absorbed
alert
curious
engrossed
enchanted
entranced
fascinated
interested
intrigued
involved
spellbound
stimulated

INSPIRED
amazed
awed
wonder

EXCITED
amazed
animated
ardent
aroused
astonished
dazzled
eager
energetic
enthusiastic
giddy
invigorated
lively
passionate
surprised
vibrant

EXHILARATED
blissful
ecstatic
elated
enthralled
exuberant
radiant
rapturous
thrilled

GRATEFUL
appreciative
moved
thankful
touched

HOPEFUL
expectant
encouraged
optimistic

JOYFUL
amused
delighted
glad
happy
jubilant
pleased
tickled

PEACEFUL
calm
clear headed
comfortable
centered
content
equanimous
fulfilled
mellow
quiet
relaxed
relieved
satisfied
serene
still
tranquil
trusting

REFRESHED
enlivened
rejuvenated
renewed
rested
restored
revived

Feelings when your needs <u>are not</u> satisfied:

AFRAID
apprehensive
dread
foreboding
frightened
mistrustful
panicked
petrified
scared
suspicious
terrified
wary
worried

ANNOYED
aggravated
dismayed
disgruntled
displeased
exasperated
frustrated
impatient
irritated
irked

ANGRY
enraged
furious
incensed
indignant
irate
livid
outraged
resentful

AVERSION
animosity
appalled
contempt
disgusted
dislike
hate
horrified
hostile
repulsed

CONFUSED
ambivalent
baffled
bewildered
dazed
hesitant
lost
mystified
perplexed
puzzled
torn

DISCONNECTED
alienated
aloof
apathetic
bored
cold
detached
distant
distracted
indifferent
numb
removed
uninterested
withdrawn

FATIGUE
beat
burnt out
depleted
exhausted
lethargic
listless
sleepy
tired
weary
worn out

DISQUIET
agitated
alarmed
discombobulated
disconcerted
disturbed
perturbed
rattled
restless
shocked
startled
surprised
troubled
turbulent
turmoil
uncomfortable
uneasy
unnerved
unsettled
upset

EMBARRASSED
ashamed
chagrined
flustered
guilty
mortified
self-conscious

PAIN
agony
anguished
bereaved
devastated
grief
heartbroken
hurt
lonely
miserable
regretful
remorseful

SAD
depressed
dejected
despair
despondent
disappointed
discouraged
disheartened
forlorn
gloomy
heavy hearted
hopeless
melancholy
unhappy
wretched

TENSE
anxious
cranky
distressed
distraught
edgy
fidgety
frazzled
irritable
jittery
nervous
overwhelmed
restless
stressed out

VULNERABLE
fragile
guarded
helpless
insecure
leery
reserved
sensitive
shaky

YEARNING
envious
jealous
longing
nostalgic
pining
wistful

Section Five: Reference

Needs Chart

The following list of needs is neither exhaustive nor definitive. It is meant as a starting place to support a process of deepening self-discovery and to facilitate greater understanding and connection between people.

CONNECTION
acceptance
affection
appreciation
belonging
cooperation
communication
closeness
community
companionship
compassion
consideration
consistency
empathy
inclusion
intimacy
love
mutuality
nurturing
respect/self-respect
safety
security
stability
support
to know and be known
to see and be seen
to understand and be understood
trust
warmth

PHYSICAL WELL-BEING
air
food
movement/exercise
rest/sleep
sexual expression

safety
shelter
touch
water

HONESTY
authenticity
integrity
presence

PLAY
joy
humor

PEACE
beauty
communion
ease
equality
harmony
inspiration
order

MEANING
awareness
celebration of life
challenge
clarity
competence
consciousness
contribution
creativity
discovery
efficacy
effectiveness
growth
hope
learning
mourning
participation
purpose
self-expression
stimulation
to matter
understanding

AUTONOMY
choice
freedom
independence
space
spontaneity

(c) 2005 by Center
for Nonviolent
Communication
Website: www.cnvc.org
Email: cnvc@cnvc.org
Phone: +1.505.244.4041

Follow-up

I'd love to read your comments and experiences with the concepts presented in the book. Send me an email at Marilyn@CoachMarilyn.com or find me at
www.twitter.com/marilynmcleod.

You'll also find the complete bibliography in this book online. I'll continue adding new books and resources as I find them.

If you've appreciated the book and would like to leave a review with your favorite online retailer, I would be grateful!

If you'd like to find a support community around the concepts of this book, please visit my website: http://www.CoachMarilyn.com. I value your contributions to the conversation about success in business and in life!

Your fellow traveler,

Marilyn McLeod
Marilyn@CoachMarilyn.com

www.ingramcontent.com/pod-product-compliance
Lightning Source LLC
Chambersburg PA
CBHW051526170526
45165CB00002B/628